Am I Gay

Phillip Lesbirel

Warning: - Language used in this book can be common words used for sexual parts of the male anatomy. Some expressions can also be thought of as crude and rude but are necessary for expressing the thought or action.

ISBN-10: 1721566678
ISBN-13: 978-1721566679

Contents

Copyright ©2016 by Phillip Lesbirel 2

Forward 4

Chapter 1 – Your own sexuality 6

Chapter 2 – Is anal sex all there is to gay sex?................12

Chapter 3 – finding a guy 23

Chapter 4 – Life as a gay man 30

Chapter 5 – Coming Out 42

Author...47

Other Books by this Author..50

Forward

This book must never be considered a reference manual or a scientific study. This book is written by a gay man and is considered his thoughts and observations and not of any medical or scientific substance. The Author is gay and what is written within these pages are his observations, his research through many online sources and in some cases, plagiarised from articles found normally on line. My interest in writing this book came from an article I read on line by Christine Webber, psychotherapist, entitled 'Am I Gay' and it caught my eye and my interest. Unfortunately, due to copyright, I am unable to show this article in this book. There are many theories pertaining to this subject; many scientific, many through University research. Some you will find are positive results of many years of research, with true scientific results, but unfortunately some are of a religious research biased towards their own religion; they find the answers they were looking for through biased data. Only the reader can decide his own sexuality. Whether the person is male or female, they are the only people who can seriously state 'I Am Gay'.

Can a gay man change his sexuality and no longer be gay? We are gay because of our own genetics and not influences around us, so even though we might hide our sexuality, marry and even have children, the stress of hiding our true sexuality seldom remains hidden and it usually bursts forth at a later time. I personally hid my sexuality for 35 years before finally coming to terms with its reality; 35 years of living a lie is hard to bare. When did I know I was a gay man? During my late teens; when I enjoyed male to male sex, Governments started to introduce laws and legislation against homosexuality and many went to prison just because they loved a member of their own sex. I was scared and sought an alternative lifestyle and married, but it was never a proper marriage and for that I apologise to my ex wife. Love is love whether it is heterosexual or homosexual. It is a love between 2 people and not a disgusting act of depravity. Sex is a beautiful act between man as a species and man's body is made to accept and enjoy sex as an act of reproduction. Our genes at conception determine who we will be; male or female. Our gender does not determine our sexual orientation but scientists theorise this occurs later in the foetal gestation. Whatever your mother's womb decides is not reversible; to be born gay cannot be reversed through prayer or medical science. We are who we are. Medical science has advanced to such a point that they can alter gender but not 100%. A man converting to a woman can have sex with a man as a normal woman can, but can never have a child as their internal body structure did not develop the ovaries to allow this when the boy was originally born: Nor women changing their gender to male, they were not born with testis, so as such, even with a full gender change, they can never produce sperm to impregnate their partner. But Nature has a way of throwing a spanner into the works of everything. There have been known to be cases of children born with both sexual organs. Their parents decide their original gender but later in life they decide their true gender and 'Gender Orientation' is performed. This usually produces a normal and happy person in their true gender.

For myself, I am happy with the gender I was given and now happy to be a gay man with all the anger thrown at me through time; I would not have had it any other way. Did I exercise my true self through sexual encounters with other men during my closet days? Yes, but seldom and only in secret; an experience I wish I never have to repeat. I hope you enjoy this book and remember; it is the observations of a gay man and not a scientific manuscript and must be treated as such.

Chapter 1 – Your own sexuality

Am I gay? This is an age old question asked by every male youth during sexual maturity. Is the love of another man just infatuation for his body, his prowess on the sporting field, the girls he tends to attract or the masculinity he oozes when he parades through the school hallways? Just because you admire him or fantasise about him in some way does not mean you are gay; quite the contrary. We all model ourselves on someone whom we admire; our father, uncle, sporting hero, maybe even a female to whom we relate to, but that does not make us gay. So what does make us consider ourselves as being a gay man? Do you fantasise when masturbating about a particular male you know, or a specific sports star; maybe a male model in a magazine hidden under your mattress, or male body builder from your body building magazine; the character in the book you are reading and see yourself as a sexual partner to him in one of the scenes? This might be your first sign to being possibly gay. Now don't get upset right now. We all fantasise in some way and about something when masturbating. We are entering a period of time when our hormones are becoming active and as yet, we have not experienced sexual activity but our body needs to practice just a little; hence masturbation. Masturbation is not a sin; it is nature's way of preparing you for life and its pleasures. Religion takes a dim view of male masturbation and so do many parents with high religious views, but how else is a man to determine if he can have sex in the first place without practicing? Don't worry; you won't wear it out so practice as often as you wish; even too many times each day if your body desires it.

Sexual desire is what drives a male forward. In nature, the male of a species is there only to procreate the species. Their testosterone levels increase when amongst females as to their pheromones and will fight other males to have the right to mate with as many females as his stamina can allow. Are we any different? We battle between ourselves for the right to procreate with a specific female; although why man has restricted himself to monogamy is another story but against nature in my opinion.

What is love? Love is an emotion driven by our own desires. It can be love of an animal, of a food, a town or city, a parent or sibling, but we always consider love to be that between two people; yes two people and not just a man and a woman. In our modern society man as a species is accepting homosexuality as an acceptable sexual deviation. However it is the more advanced Western Societies that accept it rather than 3rd world countries. Why is that? We must remember that 3rd world countries rely on their populations for their economy; their agriculture and populations to maintain those economies. Agricultural peasants work the fields mostly by hand and need extended families to bring their small holdings to become more profitable. Therefore men need to marry and produce more males for the work. Females need to marry and have children to a male. Love cannot always play a part here, so many of the marriages are arranged but still produce the extra hands to perpetuate the family needs. Homosexuality is not allowed nor condoned as that male cannot contribute to the family. These males will leave the family and seek their own kind but this is always fraught with danger.

Many 3rd world countries were part of some colonial property of a European country from the 15th and 16th century and with the colonialists came the religious zealots; the missionaries, who were mostly from the Catholic religion. They preached the word of God and demanded absolute adherence to their preaching's. This was also a time of the Inquisition and total obedience to the Holy Roman Church's law. Homosexuality; although practiced by their priests and monks, was outlawed and they demanded the colonial powers put strict laws governing these practices into the law of the land. Love is not unlawful; it is God's teaching to 'Love thy neighbour'. The Holy Scriptures were written by man for man, with man's morality of that time. The New Testament was mostly written in the 6th and 7th century by the monks of various Roman Catholic denominations. Many of the texts were removed and never used in the New Testament, so how are we to know if one of the disciples didn't write condoning homosexuality and accept it as a natural occurrence of man through the ages. Modern society throughout most western countries accepts homosexuality as the 3rd sex. However, religious groups cannot accept our 3rd sexual leaning; except 1; the Methodist Church in South Africa accepts and will marry same sex couples; a forward thinking religion.

The hardest thing for a male to do is understand and accept his homosexuality; a nasty word so from now on I will use only the word Gay; much happier sounding word and several meanings other than our use in this book. Until you experiment with sex, you cannot be 100% sure of your sexuality. Do you love to be around women or do they scare you? I was never scared of women as such, but the thought of sex with them scared the bejeavers out of me; but not with men. I was happy to search out men for sex but avoided places where women searched out men. Can men be raped by a woman or women? Yes they can; for I was one such unlucky individual; maybe it was this that finally pushed me over the edge.

Women believe they are the only ones that are raped, but in reality, a woman can rape a man and still when in a court of law demand the man raped her. I was a salesman for a trousseau company, selling these wedding trousseau chests to women at parties just like Avon or many of the other party plan products (I always enjoyed Avon parties). As I was demonstrating my wares, I noticed the women; numbered about 8, whispering amongst themselves. They then decided to play a game and I was to be included, but I was told I had to change into a costume and was dragged away into a bedroom by two of the girls and it was there they systematically groped and fondled me, and then tried to work me up for sex. I was a gay man but I was not a eunuch and after a little time, I was aroused and they then set about the sex act. It was non consensual and not looked for. If I had given any indication as to my desire for sex then I was not aware of it. I was upset and cried all night once I was on my own; I had been violated. From that day I decided that sex was for men and not women and my fate was sealed; I was then a gay man.; reluctantly or willingly? In my eyes, it was now willingly.

Your decision to seek out gay men for sex is the hardest thing your mind will ever encounter; it is against all the thinking of the norm expected of a man, or son, by parents, workmates, school classmates and society in general. Your mind has not decided what it is yet; are you gay or straight, Active or Passive. Looking for sex too has its problems; do you look in 'Cottages' or local toilets, maybe gay bars or clubs; but all are fraught with danger in some ways. Unless your local police turn a blind eye to gay men meeting in local toilets, you could be arrested if they raid it. Cottages are similar so danger there too. Gay bars are maybe the safest; although it is usual for the clientele to be experienced gay men and not all newcomers, so your naivety will show through and it is usual for the Active male to see this and approach you. Until you experience both sides of gay sex, you cannot determine your own position in relation to your own personal desires. If you like the guy first up, then go with him and experience what he offers. It is the same with gay clubs and you are likely to be picked up by an Active rather than a Passive man. However, in saying that, if you have it planned to try to be an active partner and have planned where and when, then look around and see what is parading itself around the bar or club. Then make your choice. Beware the toilet facilities at shopping centre's or Department stores. These places are usually under camera surveillance, and security guards will eject you if they see your purpose, or arrest you and pass you on to police.

My own first time was at a club. I saw a guy coming towards me and thought 'He's nice, maybe he wants me?' He did, but he dragged me into the toilet first and pashed me (heavy and consistent kissing) and fumbled my genitals. My cock rose instantly, so he dragged me into the cubical and then proceeded to excite me more, then just turned away from me, dropped his pants and I entered him. He was my first but certainly not my last. But I didn't feel satisfied after the sex; something wasn't quite right, so I waited near the toilet door and when I saw a guy I liked, entered after him and while he pissed in the trough, I groped his ass and kissed the back of his neck. He turned around while still pissing; wetting my new designer jeans, and grabbed me by the head and kissed me full on the lips. I then dragged him into the cubical and he proceeded to fuck the ass off of me. I was hooked. I wanted to be the passive from that day and so sort active partners. But you can't always pick them correctly. Some active men like it both ways, so you need to understand both ways; active and passive, regardless of your personal choices. Of course you will be nervous the first time you try to find a man for sex; that's natural, but without trying male to male sex, how can you determine if you prefer it or it was just a fantasy in your mind. Many won't like gay sex and will then know they are definitely looking for a woman for their life choice; although in time, you might graduate back towards the gay scene as your first encounter may not have been satisfying enough for you to make a choice and that first encounter scared you off for a while.

We are all different, but our needs are the same; we need to use our cocks to make love to someone or be fucked to give us the satisfaction of having had sex. Being passive does not make you any less of a man; it is just personal choice. Society puts gay men into little baskets; stereotypes if you wish: The swishing gay man with the limp wrist or the gay man whose eyes are diverted every time a young man walks through the door. Well let me assure you there is no reason for you to be stereotyped. Be yourself is what the modern gay man is all about. If art is your thing, then the swish of your hips could be the look you want to portray, but if machinery fascinates you, then being a tradesman is not against the laws of being gay; nor being an unskilled worker. Gay men practice every trade, profession and dirty job in every city on this planet; from street cleaners to mechanics to doctors to nurses or lawyers and everything in-between. You are no different to any other male and whatever you decide is your calling in life is still something a gay man can and does carry out as a job or profession. Okay, I'm back to examples now. I was a motor mechanic for 30 years and loved it. Yes I was a gay man but the unmistakable smell of grease and oil in your hair and grease under your finger nails is as much a turn on for some men as squeaky clean and smelling of aftershave.

After my marriage eventually broke down, I had several male partners who were looking for blue collar workers and not prissy boys in pink trousers. I still look for men in the trades rather than professional or white collar workers. My current partner is also a motor mechanic and diesel fitter; and African. Being gay does not limit people to European races. They are from every race on this earth. Unfortunately many of our races are known for their 'Boy-Toys' such as Thailand or Filipino. Singapore was once the capital of the 'Lady-Boy' and I assure you they were spectacular; if you wanted a boy who looked like a girl. So don't limit yourself to the guy next door look. The next Asian guy or Indian guy who approaches you may be the man you want to spend the rest of your life with under your bed sheets. Being gay is a matter of experimentation and without it, how can you be sure you have the best on offer and are happy being who you are? Try many before you make that fateful decision; but please remember; use a condom until you are sure he is clean and the man you want in your life. AIDS, HIV and VD have not been eradicated and are out there waiting for the unfortunate and reckless. Having blood tests regularly to determine your HIV status and infection to other sexually transmitted diseases is a must and should be carried out regularly; at least every 3 months. There are many community health centres that will do these tests free of charge and are very private.

Chapter 2 – Is anal sex all there is to gay sex?

Isn't that enough? Fortunately no; gay sex is as varied as it is exciting. Anal sex is what all non believers accept as gay sex but sex does not need coupling to achieve satisfaction. Anal intrusion by one of the partners is a beautiful experience, although can be a little painful to begin with for uninitiated, but you get used to it and accept it as part of the sex act. Just being close to another man; naked and fumbling each other can be as satisfying as actual intrusion. Frotage/Frottage is also another way the active partner can cum without entering your body.

Frottage - the practice of touching or rubbing against the clothed body of another person in a crowd as a means of obtaining sexual gratification.

Origin – French - It is also a word used by artists for rubbing a work of art to produce a smooth surface (are you a work of art?).

Whether you do this naked or while fully dressed is up to you. I prefer to start while fully dressed and then gradually undress and continue the act naked with my partner. Usually both partners can cum simultaneously or within seconds of each other. I assure you, your energy levels will take a few moments or minutes to rise again before you even attempt anal sex; if at all. We all consider sex as an act that ends with a climax but does that mean it must be anal for gay men? No; men can climax in many ways and does not restrict itself just to anal penetration.

Cock sucking - Have you ever sucked a man's cock? I assure you it is delightful but not something a gay man is born to do. It takes practice and the will to try, but once you experience it, you never stop. Sure the first few times make you gag a little but practice makes perfect and every gay man becomes an expert at giving 'head'. It doesn't matter if you are active or passive; the art of giving head is just as important. It is not the domain of the passive to give head. The active knows the pleasure it gives to his partner and will give it willingly.

Now we get into the more arduous methods but equally stimulating ways to 'Sexcite' a partner. The tongue, finger, a dildo and even the hand is as useful as a cock in arousal of a partner. During sexual activity, many active males will use one or more fingers up the anal passage to excite his partner. The Perineum is located just inside the anal passage and is as much a sexual organ as is the penis. The stroking of this area during kissing and stroking of the penis excites the passive partner; try it yourself when masturbating. Just a little spit on your middle finger and slide it in; now stroke the inside of your ass; get your finger in as far as possible, even more than one if you feel like it.

Dildo - A dildo is a sex toy, often explicitly phallic in appearance, intended for sexual penetration or other sexual activity during masturbation or with sex partners. The shape of a dildo can excite the perineum as much as a cock up your ass. It is a great tool to use while masturbating, but start small first and build up to larger and stranger shapes. A little lube goes a long way, so smother the dildo with lube, slide it in and while masturbating, move it about inside you. Some dildo's can be made to act as a cock ring and encase the lower part of your cock and balls, thus giving your cock some reluctance to spew forth until it can no longer hold it in. The ring is attached to an anal stimulator which when moved about inside you will act like a finger or a simple dildo and stimulate the perineum. **Warning**: - do not put anything up your anal passage you cannot remove with ease; it can be rather embarrassing when you attend the emergency section of your local hospital to remove the item lodged inside your anal passage. Believe me, even though medical records are sacrosanct; whispers of your endeavours will always reach your friends; somehow.

Fingers – As a movable object, the finger is paramount to enjoying the sexual act. The sphincter is as much a sexual organ as your penis. The feel of a finger sliding (with the aid of some lube) across your sphincter and rubbing it gently then penetrating it is an unbelievable feeling. The finger only goes as deep as the active partner wants it to go, but usually it will stroke your perineum deep inside you and cause your cock/penis to rise to the occasion. A wet finger in the ear is also sexually inviting, and you may find the smell of the finger under your nose after having been withdrawn from the anal passage quite stimulating. The smell is of your own masculine smell or musk.

Tongue – Besides the tongue being essential to explore your mouth during kissing, the use of the tongue all over the body is a must; and that includes licking the ass and pushing the tongue inside the anal passage (remind me to tell you about your personal hygiene later in the book). Most first timers have a dislike to even try ass licking. Swallow your pride and try it; in fact try everything, then make your mind up as to what you like, dislike and absolutely have to have. A wet tongue inside your ear is also delightful. Admittedly some people do not enjoy this so it's your choice, but let your partner try it a few times before you say no.

Fisting – Not something for the feint hearted, but some initiates take to it like a fish to water. Fisting, handballing, fist-fucking, brachiovaginal, or brachioproctic insertion is a sexual activity that involves inserting a hand into the vagina or rectum. Once insertion is complete, the fingers are either clenched into a fist or kept straight. As I said, it is not for the feint hearted, but if done by an expert, can be very satisfying for the receiver (again personal hygiene is paramount). The active partner lubes up his arm to almost the elbow, and then puts his hand into an arrow shape with the fingers straight out; usually with 3 or more fingers to start with. The anal passage is also well lubed with a substance usually called 'Boy Butter' or in some cases just a simple grease or lard. The fingers are then pushed into the anal passage slowly, then further in until the sphincter opens sufficiently for all fingers to enter. Once they are into the anal passage, the remaining fingers enter. Once all the fingers are inside you, the hand is then pushed inside and once this has occurred, the wrist is less of a problem; like a dildo, the wrist is like the narrow part of the dildo so enters easily. Once the fingers and hand are inside, the active partner can then massage the perineum or ball his fist and pump his fist inside you against your lower and upper bowel. I have had this done to me several times, but to be honest, I prefer just a penis. Fisting is not for everyone, but some can't get enough of it. They get off on it.

Nipples – As much a part of the male anatomy as it is for women. Sucking a man's nipples sends most into delirium; but not all. It is the act of a child feeding from its mother and is highly erotic between male and female partners but equally so for same sex partners. Some men enjoy their nipples being bitten; some quite hard. Nipples are also a sexual organ of a man; often used extensively in light and heavy bondage (that's another story for later in the book). No sane gay man would ignore his partner's nipples during cavorting in sexual embrace.

The Body – A gentle hand exploring the parts of a male body is a sensual act. Moving the hand up the thighs of your partner says you want what is between his legs. Gentle movement of your hands around his torso is as much a sexual act as the penetration, as it is telling your partner you want to explore his upper torso; his mouth, his nipples, his ears, his neck, his muscles. Every part of the male body has some significance to the sexual act. The sensual feel of a man's hand exploring your body, while you explore his is part of what you might call the 'The pre sexual act'. It is what your body responds to, and awakens it to his body and desires.

Kissing - To kiss a man is no different to kissing a female. It is what the mind and body react to prior to the sexual act. For a first time, kissing a man may feel unnatural, but that won't last for long. If you are truly a gay man, the kiss; deep and meaningful on the mouth and ears, then neck and even the nose becomes sensual and you will want more. If the guy kissing you wants more, he will undo your top buttons of your shirt and explore your chest and breathe deep the musk of your upper body; do the same to him and take a deep breath of what his body has to offer. Are you still sure you want to try gay sex? If you find your body reacts to his kisses, then follow his lead; maybe towards the toilet and explore this man. Warning: - you have just met this man, so stay within the bar or club on this occasion. If you like this man and he excites you, then dream about him when masturbating for a few days and get his phone number; give him yours and maybe make a second date. What you miss out tonight still awaits you the next time you meet. There is one difference between kissing a girl and kissing a man. Depending on the state of his beard, you might get a little gravel rash the first few times, so buy some moisturising crème for men, and use it on your face twice a day; you will get used to it in time; and remember to use a condom if having sex with someone you have never met before.

The male body was built for sex; it has no other purpose in the scheme of things, but man is more robust, more muscled and stronger than his female counterpart. He is usually taller and stronger and broader in the shoulders and thinner in the waist and hips; for obvious reasons. Some females may take me to task about that statement, but basically man started out the provider in our hunter-gatherer society and thus had to have the muscles to carry heavy animals he had caught, fight opposing tribes in defence of his family and tribe, and generally procreate with his chosen female. His strength enabled him to use weapons to kill meat for food and to kill his enemy; to travel vast distances even at running pace to get the kill. In our hunter-gatherer society the females looked after the children, dug up roots and vegetables, picked berries and generally cooked and cleaned for their family. It is only in the last 50 years of society that women have deserted the kitchen and home for the working life; not because they wanted to but life became expensive and two workers enabled the family to have what they needed. Today it is a natural thing for a woman to look at a career once the family is in school. Our standard of living increased because of what was available to us against what we expected in the past; mobile phones, TV, music on the go, cars, homes, the internet; the list is endless. Education too has changed. Women seldom had more than a basic education in days gone by, but modern society has allowed women an equal education and therefore the chance to select a career rather than being a stay-at-home mother.

Feet – Feet are a fetish; their smell, their feel on your body, the socks worn by your partner, the smell of his boots as he takes them off. Many gay men get off on the smell of feet; sucking their partners toes, licking the feet, using their partner's boots almost as a mask to breathe through. For some the smell of boots and the feet that have wore them are as much an aphrodisiac as maybe Ginseng or Viagra. For your partner to walk over your back or to push the feet into your mouth or under your nose is; to some, heaven. In some circles, licking the boots clean from cum or the soles of the boot are an integral part of their scene or relationship.

Gob – as in spit; it is used as a form of control. The active partner in say a bondage scene or slavery scene will use gob or spit as a humiliation. Some passives enjoy the humiliation and seek more. Some enjoy taking his Master's spit into his mouth and swallowing it. Don't ever discount anything unless you have tried it and decided it is not for you.

Slavery – Practiced in every corner of the gay and heterosexual world; whether it be within the leather scene, rubber scene, skinheads, bondage or many of the other fetishes; including wet sex and diapers. There are two general types of slavery; consensual and non consensual.

Consensual is where two or more parties agree to the slavery with conditions whether it is a written contract or not. The Master will abide by the agreement and a safe word is always given and if used, all contact and whatever is happening ceases. It could be agreed on for the slave to remain as a slave for a period of time; weekend, day, night, week; as agreed. When you sit down with a Master and decide what it is you want out of this slavery, put limits on what the Master can do. Can he bind you with ropes, put you in chains or shackles, cage you, imprison you; make you a pet animal for the time of your enslavement? A genuine Master is as law abiding as he is honest and he will abide by your limits; but just in case, get it in writing. The document has no real legal benefit, but it is a sort of contract between you and the Master.

Non-consensual is harder to explain as neither partner has made any commitment. Non- consensual slavery is just that; you have not agreed to being a slave or enslaved and as such anything that happens to you is illegal. Any penetration is regarded as rape. This type of slavery can occur when you consent to go home with a Master and he then places you into some form of bondage and then restricts you from leaving. The drug Rohypnol is a common drug used by these men. It is usually administered in a drink and causes the person to fall into a deep sleep and be unaware of any violation of their body. In some cases, the Master will lock the slave in a cage or a homemade prison cell and hold him for some time; even indefinitely. These are rare cases but are known to happen, so make sure you know who you are dealing with.

Many Masters can be found on gay chat lines and it is always best to find a bit about them before you commit to a session with them. Try and meet them for a coffee and then decide if he is the man you want to show you the ropes, so to speak (no pun intended). I always prefer to have an advanced meeting before I decide if I want to have any form of relationship with the man; as a Master or just casual sex. Genuine men will usually agree to a meeting, either at a local coffee shop or a gay bar. If you don't like his looks or his manner, then be polite and go your separate ways.

Prison – Many gay men dream of imprisonment. Many dream of being in prison as a genuine inmate, but do not want the conviction of a genuine crime. Many Masters have small prison cells in their bondage cells; some even have genuine ex convicts as cell mates for you. There are a few prisons where you can buy time as a convict without a conviction, but be careful here, for what happens in a genuine prison can leave you imprisoned for the rest of your life. A genuine paid prison sentence places you inside a prison with the general population in many cases. These are usually paid periods of 3 months or more; if you can afford it. These are usually in privately controlled prisons and do not come under Governmental control.

Depending on the time of imprisonment you have paid for, depends on whether you are placed in a cell with a normal prisoner, a paid ex prisoner or into the general population. Being placed into the general population can be fraught with danger, but will give you the real feelings of being a genuine convict without the registered conviction. Fights, rape, stabbings etc occur in normal prisons so it is expected that to be placed into the general population of the prison will leave you open to these actions. If this is what you really want, then go for it, but if you find a Master with a private prison, then this is a much safer option. Search the internet for private prisons where you can buy time and make sure there is a full proof contract of release at the end of your imprisonment; they are available mostly in the USA. You will be treated as a genuine prisoner and subject to all rules and regulations. Depending on what you pay for, may have you put on a chain gang and used for outside work on roads or cleaning up of local parks; but that is what you want isn't it?

Lycra – Self explanatory really; the love of all things Lycra. Tight fitting wrestling suits, bike riding gear, tight Lycra shorts, t-shirt made of Lycra to show off your bulging muscles. It is as much a part of the gay scene as the other fabrics.

Wrestling – is a sport commonly carried out by all men of any sexual persuasion. In the gay scene it is common and many groups have formed just to be able to sweat, grapple and squirm with another man. It can be carried out with wrestling suits or even naked. I prefer it naked.

Football – Football has many codes depending on where you live, but there is something sensual about a man in a sporting uniform. Soccer (English football for those in the UK) has many gay teams and they are top of their leagues. There is also naked gay football teams and they have regular matches against other gay teams. Football covers Rugby, League, American Football, Gallic football, Australian Rules, Australian League, Indoor football and many others, so if you are sports minded, there is surely a gay football team or sporting body close to where you live.

Think of a sport and there will be a gay club for you to join. Most gay bars will have them listed on their notice boards, or find a gay information site on the web for your area. These information sites will list most of the gay groups that operate in your vicinity; from gourmet dining groups, to older men's groups (if you like older men), sporting bodies, naked men's groups (if being naked is your thing), gay dance nights, transsexual groups, support groups, leather groups, rubber groups, bears; the list is endless, even groups for specific gay nationalities. Use the web and seek the information you want. It's free and available, so don't feel you are alone in this world. There are as many other youths and older men seeking answers.

Leather – The most common scene in the gay fetishes. Many gay bars or clubs will have specific nights at least once a month for leather nights and strict dress rules apply. You must wear something leather to be allowed to enter. Leather pants or tight leather jeans, leather harnesses or vests, Uniforms of police in all leather are common so are cat suits (all in one overalls) and of course the obligatory hat; peaked cap for active/Masters or baseball cap for cubs and passive (all in leather of course). There are also several deviations from the norm. Some leather slaves will arrive with their Master dressed in tight leather outfits with a dog mask and be on a lead; dog or puppy slaves; others as ponies. The theme is leather and there are no bounds to what can be worn.

Rubber - Tight fitting latex rubber is sensual and a large part of the gay scene. In many gay clubs it can be part of the leather scene so leather nights can also include rubber. It tends to be a large part of the consensual slavery scene where the passive is dressed as an animal or a slave with a collar and lead; usually hooded and led around by its Master on a dog lead. Rubber is heavily used in the Wet Sex scene; for obvious reasons.

Skinhead – A masculine part of the gay scene and considered by many to be the select few who have come from the working class gay men of the city. Their clothing is rugged and their shaved heads quite menacing. Their whole existence is based on drinking into oblivion, dancing their unique way (called stomping), their anarchy against anything institutional like Governments; and football. This is a generalisation and must be taken as such. I myself have been an active skinhead since a nipper so I consider them my brothers. However, White Power or Nazi skinheads are not true skinheads as true skinheads are not prejudiced against colour creed or race; they are what is known as SHARP (skinheads against racial prejudice). As I said, I am a skinhead and my partner is African and as black as the ace of spades. The skinhead movement came out of the West Indian migrants who originally entered the UK in the 50's when many of the colonial countries were given independence. They worked the docks of England and had a distinctive mode of dress, music and culture. The working class lads of England adopted their ways and their dress. Their music was Reggae and became their music of choice. Their uniform or mode of dress was high top boots (to stop grain and coal dust from entering their boots) their work pants were shortened and they usually wore braces to hold up their pants. Skinheads used this in the beginning but have now modified these items to include polo shirts, denim jeans with rolled up legs, high topped boots, braces and MA1 jackets of varying colours. Their heads are always shaved. In some cases short sleeved shirts with buttoned down collars are used for nights out.

Military – The military men in the gay scene tend to be part of the skinhead groups and usually will be allowed entry into skinhead nights at a gay club. Their clothing is obviously military; Disruptive pattern uniforms (DPU), or khaki pants, military steel capped boots, army shirts and jackets.

Diapers – Many gay clubs have diaper days or nights. These sessions allow men to be dressed in their diapers only, or with waterproof pants, some wear adult baby clothes such as onzies or boys clothing; school uniforms, and always with a diaper/nappy under their clothing. Daddies also attend these sessions and this is where daddies and adult babies can come together.

Wet Sex – As this suggests, it is the use of urine as a basis for humiliation. Usually part of the rubber scene, some men will spend all night in special wet areas of a club and wait for others to piss all over them, drink their piss or piss into their nappy/diaper. Some will be dressed in all rubber and have a funnel attached to their head mask and invite all others to piss into the funnel. Others will invite men to enter them and piss inside of them. They enjoy this activity and there are plenty of others who will oblige their fantasy.

Whatever your fantasy, there is a gay club that caters for it. Check out your local scene to find where to go, and immerse yourself in the scene.

Chapter 3 – finding a guy

When trying to find a partner for the night or for casual sex on a regular basis, don't look for the perfect man. Look for someone you have something in common so at least you have something to talk about. There is nothing worse than meeting someone and sitting there all night sipping your drink or coffee. Talk; find something in common. Is he a blue collar worker like you, or maybe a white collar worker but down the ladder somewhat? Is he a professional man or maybe a truck driver; a student? I'm sure you checked out his profile, so discuss his profile and dig a bit deeper. Did his photos on the profile do him justice or has he found a photo of some gorgeous male model and used that? There are many tricks used to spur your interest in him. If he is not what you expected from his profile photos, what is he hiding? Maybe it's time to finish the coffee and have to catch the next bus home?

You will meet many men before you meet a man that interests you. Sometimes, the man you weren't keen on turns out to be fantastic in bed, so don't discount them all; and any way, you're new to this, so try him out just for the experience: Experience; the age old adage for practice makes perfect. No newcomer can be perfect at his first try, so allow the more experienced to show you a few tricks, then try these out with your next conquest. Let your head go if and when you decide to go all in. Relax and let nature take the upper hand. Your body knows what to do, but your mind is reluctant, so just let the body rule in this case.

Gay chat lines like Groper or Gay Romeo, Gay Dating, or Gay Man are great to hone your skills at chatting to other gay men. If you like someone a little more than the others and want to chat privately, invite him onto maybe Skype (or other free chat systems) and you can be a little more personal. With Skype, you can video chat so you know who you are looking at and so does he. Gay chat lines are great for sifting through the thousands of other desperate men looking for a guy for the night or just for friends. Firstly, look for someone in your vicinity; no good if he lives 300 miles away or in another country. You want a fuck tonight not next year. Be ready to instantly dive out and meet him, so have a shower and clean yourself up before you start looking; that is if you are really desperate for a shag or fuck; I assure you if he is as desperate as you, he already has the car started and warming the engine up.

What do you look for when you see a profile you like? Check when he was last on line at the chat line; how many visitors he has and how many 'Likes' he has been given. This will show you his popularity. The more likes the more likely he plays the scene quite often, so be wary as sexual diseases are common place. Mind you, I have found some of the less visited profiles quite interesting and have made some very good friends from these people. Also, check out who his friends are; check their profiles too. This will show you what he is looking for as a friend or casual sexual friend. It will also show the type of fetishes he is into. Once you give him a wink or message him, he will check you out too and do exactly the same. If you are looking to hook up that night, then don't look at profiles of men who are not on line. Those on line are looking for sex; preferably for that night. That doesn't mean you ignore those not on line; they are possible hook ups for another night, but if your cock is itching, then look at those on line only. Like what you see? Are you having a wank right now; shit man, you need it all for that night of unbridled passion, not over a picture on a computer monitor, so put it away and save it for later. Now hint at a meeting that night and see what happens.

Personal hygiene is extremely important for gay sexual encounters. Your body must be clean but not smelling of soap, so use a non perfumed soap. Your ass must be clean and before you shower, have a good shit, then flush your ass out with water so the innards are squeaky clean; nothing worse than an active partner pulling out of your ass and flooding the bed sheets with your inner waste. There are plenty of products available in adult shops for this purpose, such as special shower heads you can easily attach to your shower, or cheap enema bulbs for a quick clean up in a hurry. Clean your teeth again before you leave the house and don't eat or smoke before meeting him; unless you know he smokes. There are several products you can buy from Adult Shops that freshen your crutch area; they usually call it 'Balls Fresh'. Don't ask, I've never used it. Make sure your undies are clean and fresh and decide if you wear an athletic supporter style, tighty whities or maybe tight trunk or boxer style. Your conversations with your intended sexual partner on the chat line would have determined his likes and you want to impress.

Now, clothing: It is intended that you are going to get laid tonight, so everything depends on what you wear. Tight jeans are great but hard to get off in the love tryst. Boots that cannot be removed quickly stop the pants from being ripped off. Belts are a pain in the proverbial. Shirts with a million buttons make life hard and likely to be ripped off in the melee that follows if you have an urgent desire to fuck his brains out.

Pants – tight if you want, but ever thought of buying pants with Velcro sides so they are quick to remove? No hassles with boots then either.

Boots – lace up style steel cap are always a great look, but hard to get off in a hurry. However, there are steel cap work boots that have a zip on the side, so they look like lace up boots but easily removed. However, boots worn during gay sex is not unheard of so they may not have to come off.

Belts – try finding a pair of braces; easy off in a hurry to disrobe.

Shirts – Snap studs are great for those frantic moments when the blood is boiling and the moment is nigh.

T-shirts – Great for instant removal but must have some form of connotation regarding gay sexual innuendo.

Singlets – Hope it is a warm night; little chance to take off a coat in winter and maintain that huge horn.

A lot depends on who your partner is. As a skinhead myself, there is a uniform skinheads must wear to be accepted as one of them, so a pair of tight Levi 501's around your ankles, boots still on and the rest in full use is common. So give your clothes a good piece of thought as to what you want from your night out, and dress for the occasion; dress to kill guys (sexually that is).

Again, you have to know what is in store for you that night. It's of no good wearing your best suit if you are having a night of wet sex. Rough and tumble is better suited to your old, faded, worn out jeans with no knees and holes in your ass. Bondage? Pants and a shirt; forget the undies and freeball: You ain't going to be wearing anything anyway, but boots are still a must. Your dress must reflect what it is you will expect when you finally meet up with your intended partner for the night. If it is for diaper fun, then wear a diaper under your clothes and take several in a bag with you so he can fill your diaper then change you. Make sure that if you like crèmes or lotions on your butt when being changed, you take them with you; oh and also some wet wipes.

Gay sex is not just running out and having sex. You still have to think before you act; your dress, your freshness (if that is what you have determined about your intended partner for the night). He might be into man-smells so a shower is out of the question and wear the undies you have already worn 4 times this week and covered in skid marks. Raunchy socks and the boots you wore to work, covered in grease and cow shit. Your work shirt and pants that you have worn for 3 days and stand up in the corner of your room waiting for you to put them on for one more day. Everything is relative; everything depends on what you are going into. If you are going to meet a guy who is a lawyer or a doctor, then unless he specifically asks you to wear your dirty work clothes, then for heaven's sake wear your wedding or funeral suit.

Okay, you have had your fill of the cheap guys from the dating site. Your cock is still hard and itching, and you can't find a hook up. Time to take your future into your own hands; not literally and have a wank; I mean get dressed how you like and head off to the local toilet block or cottage; preferably one with a couple of cars on the outside and a broken bulb in the toilet block. It will be pitch black, and hands will grope you from every angle and some will even unzip you and suck you off. Don't be alarmed; isn't that what you went there for? Try a bit of groping yourself and find someone who is not active with another and start to feel him up, then unzip his fly and let his cock flop out and start to suck him off. He may turn you around and after his cock is hard, attempt to enter you; your decision as to if you let him, but remember the condom in your pocket. Spit is a good lube but a small sachet of lube is always a good thing to have next to your condoms.

Some men prefer sex naturally and not with condoms or as they say 'A Raincoat'. If you decide you only want safe sex, then demand it. If he refuses, then walk away. There are others in the toilet block you haven't tried yet. Not all the participants are on the inside. Those who were in their car when you entered may join you. They wait until they see someone they like, and then enter. Be wary here, because some of these men are police waiting to trap you, but these days, most police turn a blind eye to cottages. It is only when the neighbour complains that they take action.

Then there is the casual acquaintance through a friend or a party. Your eyes meet over the sofa or pool and there is an instant reaction in your groin; now's the time to get aggressive and go for it. Find somewhere private and just do it; the hall cupboard, the bedroom, the laundry, the pool house, the bushes; just go for it tiger. Not seen anyone who makes your groin itch yet? Stand away from the toilet and wait. If you see a likely candidate, then move towards the toilet as he reaches the door and shove in front of him, then casually turn around and say ' there's always room for two' and see what happens. Might lead to something interesting; maybe.

It's no good being a snow flake on a hot tin roof; you will melt into the scenery. Let the other men see you. Go and introduce yourself to the guys or to their groups; be bold, they can only ignore you, but maybe one wont. You've seen the movies where boy meets girl; girl likes boy, boy gets girl. Well you are both the boy and the girl, so use your masculine or feminine charms; whichever is required. If you are at a gay party, it is not unheard of to unzip him right there in the lounge room and suck him off. He might find you a bit brazen, but you have caught his interest and I assure you he wants to find out more about you. That guy who just grabbed your ass is also interested, so turn and kiss him, then see where it leads. Being a wall flower will get you nowhere except your own little lady; your right hand.

If you find a guy and you get his phone number, it should be obvious who is going to ring who. If you get a couple of dates, then try and suggest being boyfriends. Let that fester for a while before you get real serious and really get to know him before you commit. What you see when you are having casual sex is not always what you get when living together. You may not see his jealous side when dating. His personal hygiene may not be what you expect. You might be a neat and tidy person and he is just a slob. He eats with his fingers and wipes his hands on his pants. Sometimes it's the silly things that annoy us, so don't think it is you. We all have annoying habits but when dating these are not as apparent as when sharing a flat. Does he like the kitten you bought or is he cruel to it? Do you really like that Rottweiler he so lovingly cares for, that chews your best loafers to shreds? Be sure he is the one you want to share your life with; or at least for the next 7 years, which is as long as most marriages last these days. If you have taken the plunge and decided you are definitely gay and you want to find a soul mate, then these are the things that will become important whilst dating. Find out all about him; visit his family, mix with his friends. They all know him much better than you do and they have all the nitty gritty about him; especially his mum or older sister. They know how often he has a wank as they hear his groans; change his underwear as his mum always does the washing. His sheets; does he change them weekly or when they crawl out of his room demanding attention from his mother? Is his room an absolute mess or is he tidy? Mother's know everything and yes, they also know their son is gay well before they tell her; that's the next chapter.

Still undecided if this is the life you want? Then it is time to go to a gay men's group and sit in on a few counselling sessions. Talk to the councillors and be truthful about your situation. They cannot advise you if you lie to them. Talk to some of the others in the group and find out how they realised they were gay or if they are still undecided. It may take you a long time to come to a decision, so don't hurry. This is not picking the flavour of the ice crème you want at the shop. This is the rest of your life. Once you make that decision either way, the weight comes off your shoulders, but sometimes there is still lingering doubts. Don't rush to come out and tell the world. Once the genie is out of the bottle it is hard to get him back in. Think before you act, then pick the right moment if you want to come out. How do you do that? Everybody is different and no two cases are the same; that is a problem only you can solve, but I will give you a few hints at the end of the book.

Chapter 4 – Life as a gay man

So, what would your life be as a gay man? Some individuals still hate gay men and gay bashing is still a favourite pastime for some. Recent events by crazed gunmen in the USA have proved this point, but on the whole, most people are for it or not bothered one way or another. There will always be one person who will object or start talking with innuendos about your sexual leaning. If they are work mates, then report them to your Human Resources department and demand he stops. Even family members will have the odd dig at you. But basically most won't care. However, in saying that, if you are a member of a sports team, you may find some reluctance to have you on their team. Homophobia is rife in the masculine sports and again it needs the coach to lay down the law, because if he doesn't then he leaves the team and its officials in a legal bind. There have been many great name sporting heroes who have come out as gay men in later life, but usually after their time in the limelight has gone. Ian Thorpe (swimming Australia), Carry Grant (famous male film star), Ellen DeGeneres (daytime show host), Ian Roberts (NFL player Australia) and many more. There are also many artists, writers, poets; all known homosexuals; Oscar Wilde, William Shakespeare, Emily Dickson was a known lesbian, Peter Ilyich Tchaikovsky; composer of Romeo and Juliet and the Nutcracker Suit, Kitchener, British general who Established peace in the Sudan; and the list goes on, so you are in good company if this is your lifestyle.

Many clothing designers were known to be gay such as Steven Linnard who designed many of Kyle's clothes, clothes for The Pet Shop Boys (boys band) and Boy George to name a few. Most of the high fashion women's clothing designers were gay. Being gay does not stop you and your partner having a family either. Look at Elton John or George Michael. If a country allows gay marriage then it also allows gay adoption or gay fostering.

If and when you get into a relationship, you will already know your part to be played. It is likely both of you will still work, so share the load on weekends so you can both enjoy the time together, instead of just one of you doing all the housework. As individuals, you will both have friends you cherish and like to meet, but your partner is not keen, so have one day a week where you both go out and be with your friends separately; it helps keep the peace. Try and have a dinner party once a month where you invite the friends both of you enjoy and let your hair down; maybe have everyone in a 'Super Hero' costume, or all in drag; nothing like lycra to show off ones credentials during dinner. Have fun and I'm sure your friends will have a great time too. Warning: - Don't fill the night with happy snaps of home movies; how boring. Try and keep the favoured cat or dog away in another room or out in the garden. If you have a pool, then have a naked pool party; nothing better than alcohol and water for a fun filled night.

Remember, the other 6 nights of the week will be fairly hum drum. You have both worked hard and you are tired with work the next day, so relax with the telly and a good stiff drink. If you feel like an early night, don't just sneak off; suggest your partner join you. A little tussle under sheets will give you a good night's sleep. Once you are in a relationship, both of you will have to compromise to make things work. Ordinary mundane chores still have to be done, so if it is always a tussle to get help, then suggest a house cleaner come in once a week, or if you both earn a good wage, then maybe a houseboy would be just the thing to look after the house, garden, car washing, wash the dog and maybe a 3 way some nights. There are solutions to every problem; you just have to sit and talk about it. A housekeeper for a couple of hours a week will cost less than $50, so why waste the weekend cleaning house? Go out and have brunch on Sunday with friends, go to the local gay resort or just relax. Sleep in after that raucous diner party you threw last night or that outrageous party Joe threw. I assure you housekeepers can be very silent about what they find in the bedroom. I have a housekeeper who comes in for 1 hour each week. She vacuums, washes the downstairs tiled floor, cleans the bathroom and generally keeps my place hygienically clean. I work 6 days a week and when not working, I am writing. $20 a week is well worth someone else seeing your unmentionables still laying in the dryer when she comes to clean. I do the washing and make my bed but little else so I am overjoyed when I come home on Thursdays to find the bathroom spic and span and the carpet neat as a pin. I am also a messy cook, so the kitchen is always a splattered mess and spills are constant on the kitchen floor; but I do the washing up, even if it is the morning the housekeeper is coming. To be honest, I just can't be bothered doing the cleaning. Not all relationships work out, so when you find you are starting to have regular fights or shouting matches, it is time to go home to mother; or find another flat. Don't hold out hoping it will improve, because it won't so get out now before one of you gets hurt.

The age old argument is always who sleeps on what side of the bed: Passive on the right, active on the left; husband on the left, wife on the right. Now we have that sorted, what about on the sofa? Well the active will find his spot and the passive will fit in somewhere: The TV remote? Sorry, your active partner has hidden it and soaps are for when you are alone with a box of tissues. Even as a gay relationship, you will follow the rules of normal marriage. He will pick the sport to watch on weekends; Come Dancing is for Sunday mornings early when he is still snoring; you don't consider that a sport do you? More like a gladiatorial battle of the glamorous and effeminate. I'm sure if you hint enough, that gay movie on the gay channel could be considered.

Your partner will give comments on the outfit you are intending to wear that night, but low and behold if you do the same, so zip it and save your sanity. Mind you he might be in a good mood and suggest those tight leather jeans and yellow polo shirt; hint of play to come maybe? If you are the passive you will take your lead from him; visa versa if you are the active. Life as a gay couple is seldom different to normal heterosexual couples; without the kids in most cases. But there is one danger area here and that is if your partner was married and has kids. They may or may not live with you, but you are not their father; he is. You might like them; or not, but for peace in the household, try to get to know them and get along. Nothing breaks up a relationship quicker than the kids.

While at school in your last year, you have many decisions to make and the most important is your future career. The fact that you are also undecided about your sexuality does not rate a mention when choosing your career path. Being gay does not stop you doing whatever your mind tells you to do. All jobs, trades and professions are yours for the choosing. Is it art, music, drama, as a tradesman, a doctor, a lawyer, an accountant (Oh please don't chose to be an accountant), a factory worker, shop assistant or even a council road sweeper. Who cares except you? Everything is relative. No good driving yourself to be a doctor if you are bottom of the class. No good thinking about a career as a garbage truck driver if you have good grades either. Look at your grades and aim to use what you have stored up top. Your life will be much better if you work in a job commensurate with your own brain power. Mow lawns if that's what you want to do with your life and don't let anyone else say different. It is the same with sexuality; don't let others say you are gay so go get a job as a shop window dresser. That is your decision and yours alone. It is the same with your sexuality; your decision. Nobody can tell you what you feel and are. Your job does not define your sexuality, but does define you as a person. Don't let others say you are gay so just find a guy; you have to make sure you are gay and are prepared to be the best gay man you can be: Still not sure? Don't let others push you to something you may regret later in life. It is not hard to think you are gay and find out later that you were just scared to be around women all along, and you now want to get married and have 10 kids. Oops, all your friends are now gay and the only women you know are fag-hags. Now you have to start the dating game all over but with the opposite sex.

Ever gay man has been where you are now. Every gay man has had to choose his profession, his sexuality and his partner. Don't worry, you will have many partners before the moon blinds your eyes and you fall madly in love. For some it is a lifetime and others the first guy they have sex with. Don't become discouraged. Many teenagers worry too much about who will find out they like men, or their parents will disown them; their friends desert them. For some this will happen, but that is why we have friends. These friends are your lifeline to sanity when all hell breaks loose. Get a good circle of friends you can rely on. Too many of our gay youth commit suicide because they bottle it all up inside and won't talk to others about their problem. There is always someone to talk to, but only you can search them out and make the effort to go and talk with them. They are only a phone call away, or a chat line for some. Check out the gay help groups and do something about your indecision. Meet other youth with the same or similar doubts. They will be the friends you call on when you are in trouble with your own thoughts. **Remember; YOU ARE NOT ALONE**.

You are in a long line of men who throughout the ages have gone through these thoughts and indecisions. No man wants to be gay, but our own genetics through our senses and emotions send them in opposite directions and we react to our own sex and not the opposite sex. Science has looked at this phenomenon and discovered that the sex of a child is determined by the mother and a gay child can occur in the 3rd or 4th child in a family. Twins with one gay and one normal, show this tendency. Of 4 children, I am gay and the oldest, and my youngest brother is gay; he is child number 4. But when digging into the family tree, there were other family members who were gay; both male and female when being gay was definitely taboo. Check into your own family history and I'm sure there will be an uncle your mother or father seldom mention because he was gay. Not sure how far back you can go as when I tried, there was no recorded history of stone age relatives; now that's an interesting thought, a gay stone age relative; don't go there.

Homosexuality is not something only in human beings. Same-sex pairing is not just normal in the animal kingdom - it's even common. Studies suggest that about 1,500 animal species are known to practice same-sex coupling - from insects, to fish, birds and mammals. Among giraffes, there's more same-sex than opposite-sex activity. In fact, studies say gay sex accounts for more than 90 percent of all observed sexual activity in giraffes. And they don't just get straight to business. Male giraffes know how to flirt, first necking with each other - that is, gently rubbing their necks along the other's body. This foreplay can last for up to an hour. Scientists have documented over 1500 species that display homosexual acts; now doesn't that slap a wet fish on religious doctrine

Don't go to a religious institution for help in determining your sexuality; they think only one way and will tell you it is 'Just a phase' you are going through and tell you 'pray to God' is your best way to overcome your affliction. The Mormon Church even has their own rehabilitation centres for converting their gay congregation. Every town, regional centre or city has a community health centre where you can talk with a doctor who is there to offer assistance to gay people. He can also put you in touch with groups you can find help. In Cairns where I live, they call it the 'Dolls House' where a gay man can get treatment for sexual diseases, have blood tests to determine HIV, sexual advice and much more. It is run by the State Government, but is totally secret and nobody will ever know you have been there. Search 'Gay Support Groups' on your computer and it should come up with groups in your own area. If you're having problems with bullying, then the police will have a gay liaison team who are willing to sit down and talk with you; again be frank, they have seen it all; and that includes cyber bullying through such media as Facebook, Twitter etc.

Life as a gay man is definitely not the same as your normal friends, but there again, what is normal. Society calls normal a marriage of a woman and a man, burdened with mortgage payments, a white picket fence, a station wagon, cat, dog and 1 ½ kids. Gay couples do not fit that description. They are duel income no kids; (DINKS), usually with 1 or more houses and a nice car and usually only one of the couple has a license to drive. Life for them is comfortable, but this is the stereotypical gay couple. In reality, many work low paid jobs and live alone in a 1 bedroom flat or in a boarding house. You wouldn't give these guys a second look in the street. But, as I said previously, gay men work in every field of employment, and it is estimated that 10% of the population is gay (male and female) so they have to be everywhere. Some occupations are more likely to have gay employees than others, but don't discount all occupations. Gay men are not necessarily obvious from their looks, clothing and actions. It is through casual conversation, or meeting them at a gay venue that will confirm their sexual status. Not all gay men are the metrosexual type who use face crème at night and a small amount of makeup to highlight their best points. The gay gardener is usually sunburnt face and arms and rugged features. Same with the pool boy or the supermarket delivery boy, the pizza boy; your local bus driver; any one of them could be gay. You cannot see by looking except in some obvious exceptions.

Depending on the life style you decide is yours, depends on how you dress, what you spend money on, how you eat. Sure your employment will have some bearing on this too, especially if going out with workmates. You would dress as you expect them to dress or they expect you to dress. When out looking for action for the night, you dress in a way you will attract what you are looking for. Going out to a club or gay bar is again different, this is definitely where you dress to attract not to impress. Active will dress masculine in his preferred fetish gear. Passive will also dress in their preferred fetish gear but more provocatively; tight jeans to show your ass, tight Lycra or t-shit to show your pecks.

There is also an alternative to coming out gay, and that is bisexual; having it both ways. You might find a girl you like and date her, but 1 night a week you go looking for men and that means you have decided if you are passive or active. In many cases, bisexuals prefer the passive side of gay life. They can get all the sex they need as an active with their girlfriend, but not as a passive partner, so go looking for a male sexual partner to achieve the anal sex they desire. Many gay men consider bisexual men as gay men who have not decided their sexuality yet. But this is not true. Men can crave many types of sexual encounter and while you were testing the market, you found you enjoyed anal intrusion as much as being the giver. If that's the case, then being bisexual is not a major problem. Being bisexual does not mean you are gay, but you enjoy some gay sexual encounters. You can enjoy it both ways, so you don't have to commit yourself to one life style until you are really sure it is what you want.

Your life is yours to decide. If being gay is what your heart desires, then do it and do it now. The longer you put off your decision the harder it will be. You don't have to declare your sexuality to the world until you are happy in your own mind.

You can be gay without being 'Out'. Being closeted can have advantages and disadvantages. It hides your sexuality with others you have decided need not know but allows your close friends to know. What you tell your family is up to you, but mother always knows. You know your family best so will understand any objections they may have; if any. I am aware of many men who have come out to their family who worked in masculine blue collar jobs, played football each week and drank with the boys after work. Coming out can be selective and if you want to hide the fact that you are gay, then that is your prerogative. Don't be pressured into revealing your sexuality by other gay friends. They might be out and comfortable, but you have to find your own comfort zone. If that is casual sex with males, then so be it. If gay sex is what you prefer, then casual sex is a great way to get experience and discover what you like and dislike in the scene. Gay sex is like a smorgasbord at your local club; you chose what you want and leave the rest for others. I assure you what you decide to take will more than satisfy your appetite for gay sex. Later you can experiment with other fetishes. If fetishes are not your thing, then just good old fashioned gay sex is still a pleasure.

Gay sex chat lines are a great way to find sex in your area for a night of debauchery, but there are so many guys on line and so many good looking pics of their ass, their prick or their abbs. If the guy does not have a face pick, then ask him to put one up on his profile. If he says he doesn't want to put a face pic up; then disregard him. You should always know who you are talking too and that is why Skype or Yahoo chat are very good as they have video chat. There are a lot of unscrupulous guys out there and some are just Trolls; out to get whatever they can from you. If they are not living in your area; regardless of how much they make your crutch itch, forget it. Long distance relationships are hard and fraught with danger; don't go there. Russian boys are out for what money they can get from you; and they will get it without you realising. The same goes for many of the old

Eastern Bloc countries; stay away from them. Keep your chats to guys living in your own neck of the woods. Chat lines are the best way to find out a bit about the guy you find interesting from his profile. Many profiles will tell you to 'message him if you want to know what he's into'. So how can you find out if he is the one you like? You can't, so why bother. If he doesn't have the decency to list a few of his fetishes or likes, then he could have something to hide. He sure is not the guy wanting sex tonight, so ignore him.

Gay saunas, or gay sex on premises buildings are a good place to get casual sex too. Gay sex on premises sites are usually dark and allow you to either get sucked off or suck off another guy without them knowing who you are. They usually have sling rooms if you want to have sex either way and there are always guys available for casual sex. Most; if not all, will allow their patrons to strip on entry and remain naked for the whole time they are there. They all have 'Glory Holes' and TV rooms showing pornographic movies of gay sex, just to get you in the mood.

Gay saunas are normal saunas but for gay men. Hot steam rooms, sauna rooms, cold pools and normal swimming pools. Many a gay guy has been sucked off in the steam room or sauna, and it is a healthy and satisfying place to go. Usually cost a lot more than a sex on premises site, but it is clean and usually full of guys looking for a fumble and a suck; and all naked too. You might meet the guy of your dreams at any one of these types of establishments. Many of these saunas also have massage rooms at set hours so a gay massage will relax you after a good rough and tumble in the sauna; good for relaxing after a hard day's work too. Make this a habit before you go out looking for guys at the night club. The clubs don't get busy until after 10pm anyway.

What you do while making sure you are a gay man, decides your future as a man. To make an informed decision, you need to know all the facts. Are your dreams fantasies or are they real? Are you masturbating with gay thoughts or just thoughts of random sexual encounters? You must be certain of what it is you want to live your live; gay or straight. Don't put pressure on yourself to make that decision immediately. It takes years for our own sexuality to be determined and emotions are the way our mind and body make those decisions. Some youths know their sexuality from well before their teens. Others, like yourself, are having difficulty deciding what you really are, so experiment. Go out with girls and boys and have sex both ways, then decide. Like food, you don't know what you like until you try it. Regardless of your age, there are groups who cater for you, so seek them out and talk with the councillors and the other guys in the group.

It doesn't matter if you are 14 years old, 16 years old or older. Gay organisations have groups who form weekly, monthly or when required. Their councillors are experienced social workers who understand your problems and deliberations. They are gay themselves and went through the same as what you are going through now. To ignore these groups and organisations is denying you help with a problem that can manifest into something much more dangerous like depression. Depression can kill and gay youth suicide is twice the rate of normal youth suicide; don't go there, seek help.

Youth who are trying to determine their sexuality tend to bottle it up inside themselves and feel ashamed to talk about it. This is what leads to depression. Until you sit down and talk with a qualified councillor, it will pray on your mind. Your mind will be working ten to the dozen when you lay down to sleep so your mind continues to work and give you fitful sleep and you wake up tired and grumpy. You cannot concentrate at school and your grades drop and your parents start to have a go at you. You stop eating properly and your health deteriorates. Your body becomes undernourished and that is not a good look for a gay man trying to find a partner or hook up.

If you want to take out your frustrations, then take up running, or go to the gym; take up boxing if that interests you, or cycling. Maybe kick boxing or the martial arts are more your scene, but just do something. Anyway, you can meet more guys in the gym than at home in your room, and a good body is a great advertisement for you. There is nothing better than a guys body with good pecks, washboard abbs and muscles in his shit, but not too many or you'll look like a gym queen. Your body must be fit and masculine and not puffed out unnaturally as some body builders try to achieve. Hard work never hurt anyone, so if you are not an Einstein, then a heavy manual job will keep your body fit and healthy. But I am assuming your grades are fair so maybe a trade or clerical job; maybe University?

So much depends on you. If you bottle everything up, then your self esteem drops and you head downwards and look for jobs that are in keeping with how you feel about yourself. You need to make that decision and be happy with it and then decide what you are going to do with your life, and go for the best you can be; it's not that hard if you are a good student. You know what your limits are and nobody else does: Poor or middle of the road school results don't send you to the bottom of the job market. Now is the time to sell yourself to employers; maybe you will find a gay Human Resources Manager and fuck your way into a good job, but don't bank on it.

You are who you are and if you find your grades are low or middle of the road, then look for a trade then leave school and start learning how to work and earn a living. School is for those who want to avoid work as long as possible or for those with good grades and want to go further. Many of our greatest entrepreneurs had poor schooling but had brilliant minds. Most of our greatest builders and tradesmen had limited schooling in the 50's and 60's and went on to start their own building business and expanded over the years to become major players.

Okay, you have read this far, so I am going to say you have already made up your mind; now you want to find out a few home truths and have some questions answered. So I am gay, what now? Accept who you are and get on with life. Your new life has just begun and it can be a rewarding and happy experience. You now realise you will never marry and have children, so get on with finding the right mate for you. It's time to go out and find a guy for the night and start experimenting with gay sexual encounters and finding out what turns you on; gives you that sexual excitement. Is it rough sex, or is it a tradie? Are you excited by the thought of bondage or consensual slavery? Are you fascinated by wet sex and all its connotations? Dress for your fantasy and go either to the clubs or to the local cottage and find that man.

Chapter 5 – Coming Out

Do you need to come out as a gay man? That will always be your choice. It is normal for a guy to take his latest girlfriend home to meet mum. If mum doesn't see a girl friend at Sunday lunch then she is going to ask awkward questions, so maybe you should sit her down and tell her the truth; she will help you come out to the rest of the family. If your family is religious, then coming out may cause problems, so keep it under your hat for a while until you figure something out. In most cases, your sexuality will not cause too many concerns at home. Your father may feel cheated but you mother will understand more quickly. Brothers and sisters quite likely suspected anyway, so no big surprise. Your biggest problem will come from religion, especially if your family are devout in some of the more fanatical religions like Mormon or Muslim, even Salvation Army or Catholic. Religion has decided over the centuries that homosexuality is a sin; a sickness to be cured and prayed for. If you relate to those religions, then coming out will cause a rift within your family, so be prepared to find your own home and place in an area where gay people tend to be more active. You now have to take your life in your own hands and live it as you believe is best for you. You can still practice religion but you can't come out as this will cause problems between you, your family and their religious beliefs. As a gay man, you will always need a support base behind you; family or friends or both. Friends understand your way of life, your family know you but not your way of life so support comes from those who understand your problem best.

If you know you will never be happy until you come out to the world, and you are worried about your family, then go and get counselling. In some cases, the councillor will even assist you to come out; be there when your big day comes and basically support you. When I came out at 18 years old to my parents, they were born again Christians, but they accepted my life choice very well. They did question me about my choice but accepted it. It did take several years before it was a comfortable subject at the Sunday lunch table. After 50 years it is a comfortable time at home and openly talked about; especially now my youngest brother has also come out as gay. He has also married his lover and they now a comfortable life together. My marriage to my ex wife did throw a spanner into the works for a while, but once I divorced, my parents were happier and preferred my male lovers to my ex wife. They are still very religious but are for gay marriage. To them, love is between two people and not a man and woman.

My other surviving brother is a little homophobic and his wife definitely is. My youngest brother lived within a short distance from them when he was in his early 20's but they seldom invited him to their home. It was an unnecessary act by a brother but he decided marital bliss was more important to brotherly love. This may be a choice you might have to make with some of your family members.

Coming out at work is also fraught with danger. I had been a member of the military for 15 years when gay men were allowed to be recruited, but because I had spent my entire military life as a heterosexual, to come out would have destroyed my career. In the military, you depend on the people above you to recommend you for promotion. If I had come out, I would have been seen as a liar and a cheat for the last 15 years, so kept my peace until about 12 months before I had decided to retire. I went to the Base Chaplain and confessed to my homosexuality. His reaction was as I expected and he immediately ordered me to attend Bible Study that lunch time. It was an order, so I went to the base chapel at the time suggested. He met me at the door and told me to go into the meeting room. I entered the room and saw about 12 other guys, so found a spare chair and sat down; not knowing what to expect. Finally the chaplain entered the room then announced he was going to a base meeting and for us all to get to know each other, then casually stated that we were all gay men together. I'm sure he saw our jaws drop as he said it, and sure enough every man in the room was gay. During the remaining 12 months of my career, I met several gay military men and my life became more enjoyable. It was good to know you were not alone.

Coming out at work always depends on your relationship with your fellow workers. In this modern time, being gay is no longer a major issue as discrimination by other employees is strictly governed by law for most western countries. It is those countries that have laws against homosexuality where you have to be careful. If you have decided you are definitely gay, then be gay from the first day you start work. Let your fellow workers know; it doesn't matter what job you are doing. It is better to put up with a few innuendos at the start than be rejected at a later date when you decide to come out.

I run a small non registered charity in an African country where there are laws against gay men. I train unemployed gay youth in the trade of motor mechanics; a masculine trade where they can hide their sexuality through their work choice. All my employees are gay youth. I supply them with a living wage which as an apprentice with other workshops is nonexistent, and they survive on tips from clients. These youths also have to buy their apprenticeship and buy their release after its completion which few can do, as they don't get paid so cannot save enough to be released so work for their whole lives unpaid.

I also supply them with work clothing and safety gear; including work boots. I also supply them with an individual tool kit and a place to live. I train them, educate them at their equivalent to a trade school so they have a qualified trade they can use anywhere. I also supply a covered workshop area, vehicle driving licenses and push bikes for them all. Recently I bought them a washing machine so they can wash their uniforms and not have to wash them by hand. The advantage of this workshop for gay men is that each are gay and therefore can be themselves at all times. Two of the apprentices sleep at the workshop in a container I purchased and had renovated to make two separate rooms with proper beds, a mattress and bedding, as well as a proper toilet, shower and kitchenette, as well as a TV and a lounge. It doesn't cost much of your western wage to help these boys. It cost me about 10% of my weekly wage.

It is important that you feel comfortable about being gay at home, your workplace and with friends. Your life is therefore normal. It is only when you come across homophobia that things can become uncomfortable. Only you can overcome this either by direct intervention with that person, or through your Human Resources office. Don't let it go; nip it in the bud before it goes too far. A workplace that is uncomfortable will ultimately force you to leave and your reputation will follow you, so stop the innuendoes and humiliation immediately. You like your job and discrimination has no place in modern society. It is the person who is making your life uncomfortable that has to change, not you. He or she has to understand that society has changed and it is high time they changed too.

I hope I have helped you decide in some small way. Remember, this is a guide only and you need to consult others with the expertise to guide you to make your decision with well informed advice. I am a gay man who has gone through the same indecisions as you have; although at a more precarious time, but I have never regretted my decision to come out as a gay man; it is better than the alternative. Living as a gay man is no different to living as a heterosexual man; other than a wife instead of your own husband. You can pick any career of your choosing; whether it be a trade, a profession, or just a manual job; the choice is yours and yours alone. Being gay does not stop you being anything you desire, and one thing a gay couple has over heterosexual couples is potential wealth. If you both work and earn a decent living, apart from the statuary Superannuation fund, you can save for your retirement by investing in property. Holidays together overseas is also highly probable. Unless you decide to foster or adopt children; or your partner has already got children, then your earnings are yours to do with what you want; children will always keep you poor, but also happy.

Don't be afraid to be gay. Being gay is as much a masculine thing as having 10 kids; only your sexual encounters are more varied and more enjoyable for most of the time. Gay sex is not unnatural as most people will have us think. Animals do it regularly and we are as much a part of the animal kingdom as they are, so do your own thing and to hell with anyone else. Practice safe sex; make sure your body and internals are clean; dress for the occasion; be sure of who you meet; and have a safe and enjoyable life. Being gay is not something you choose to be; remember, it is what you are, so enjoy it.

Author

Phillip Lesbirel is a prolific writer with over 50 novels to his name at time of this publication. He lives in Cairns in Far North Queensland, Australia, and works as a public bus driver. His novels cover a multitude of subjects and genre. He is a known SHARP (Skinhead Against Racial Prejudice) and has not hung up his boots just yet and has several Skinhead books to his name.

Phillip is a gay man, and is partnered to Peter. Peter has been his partner since 2012 and is from Ghana; although born in Liberia, he became a refugee in 1992 during the civil war in Liberia at the age of 5 years. His family were massacred but he was rescued by a family friend and taken over the border to Ghana: That was where Phillip met Peter. His spare time is always writing books to add to his collection. He writes of his experiences and his dreams and aspirations as a gay man. His furtive mind knows no bounds when it comes to a story line and he often uses the many gay fetishes as part of his stories but gay romance is always top of his thoughts.

Phillip spent 22 years in the Royal Australian Air Force (RAAF) as a Ground Support Fitter (Motor Mechanic and Diesel Fitter) and would still be there had not he reached compulsory retirement age. On his trip to Africa in 2012; where he met his partner Peter, he saw the terrible conditions under which apprentice motor mechanics were trained and treated, and decided he could help even just one youth to be well trained. He opened a small workshop and took on an apprentice. Peter was already qualified as a mechanic so took on the duties of training this apprentice. Over the next 6 years, he has employed 4 other apprentices and paid for each to attend the local Trade Training establishment; the Tema Technical Institute (TTI). He has also trained one youth who was illiterate to qualify as a mechanic and set him up in his own workshop in his own village. This dedication to helping these youth is at his own expense and is not a recognised charity. It is run under the name of Trade Training for African Youth through the workshop in Tema in Ghana called CKL Mechanical Services (Coffee Kofi and Lesbirel Mechanical Services). As gay men are persecuted in Ghana, the apprentices he sought to train were all gay youth and allow them to be themselves at work and to be able to earn a living as gay men. Most gay men in Ghana are very masculine as to be effeminate would see them imprisoned for up to 5 years..

Hole in Time is a book about a youth who accidentally falls through a hole in time and becomes his ancestors. He travels through different periods of time yet when he returns to his own time, he has been gone but seconds, yet remains with his ancestors for months and sometimes many years. He learns about his heritage and finds out he is of Aboriginal heritage. He keeps the knowledge of his ancestors and their skills and when he finally returns to his own time, searches out his Aboriginal heritage through an aunt of his fathers who is Aboriginal and an elder of her tribe.

When they meet, she insists he be taken into her tribe and is put through the 'Coming of Age' ceremony and through this, he becomes the Keeper of Stories for his tribe. But he knows from his passage through time that he comes from another world and discovers his heritage lies in Tasmania. With his family, they head for Tasmania and he builds his home and business there. His land where he builds his home was once sacred land of his ancestors and the trees he used for the house are the spirits of his ancestors as well as the stone he uses. These spirits visit him and lead him to a life dedicated to bringing back the Aboriginal people to their land. It is through him that the Aboriginal people of Tasmania educate themselves and become members of parliament and gradually take their land back. Their move to reassert themselves in their traditional lands do not go unnoticed by the Far Right, and when the Aboriginal elders decide to hold a Corroboree, the Patriotic Youth League attack the meeting and several people are injured and 3 killed; but through hard work, the Aboriginal people of the Palawa Tribe gradually take their lands back from the White Invaders. May 3rd each year becomes a Public Holiday to remember their dead.

.

Other Books by this Author

Gay

Growth of Love – Two men of different backgrounds meet in a men's hostel and fall in love.

Hi are you there? – An occult story of a spirit; the spirit of a man who has been in a coma for over 20 years, finding his boyhood love

A Collection of Short Stories, One Act Plays and a Christmas Carol

The Carer – A gay man finds love with a man who has an unusual job; looking after those about to die but spiritually. Is he a Guardian Angel?

The Gay Mechanic – A gay youth who wants to become an apprentice mechanic. Can a gay man be successful in a masculine world?

The Right to Live – Outed as a gay youth at school and thrown out by his father, a youth runs away to find his own life and becomes entangled with prostitution and drugs. He finds true love from an unusual source but his lover is reported killed in a motor accident and his life turns to despair.

We were straight - Two family men meet at a single father's guidance meeting and decide to help each other with their families; not realising they would fall in love. They decide to combine their families but life always turns to something unexpected.

To Be Reborn – Marshal was imprisoned for a crime he didn't commit, but his father believed he did and wiped his hands of his only son. His love of an Afro-American youth led to their living together but Marshal managed to steal the fortune of an underworld gang. Marshal changes the colour of his skin with a leather dye and with his partner Zac, try and hide in Canada, but are discovered.

Life in Black – Billy was a white boy from the wrong side of the tracks in Chicago. He ran with a black gang as they had all grown up together in the same trailer park. The gang decided to do an armed robbery at a local service station to get money to go out that night, but it all went wrong. Two men were killed and Billy was arrested for murder; he had been caught on CCTV. The deputies knew Billy well from his troubled youth and this time they decided to get rid of him for good. They organised a hot bath for him; a hot bath of a strong dark brown leather dye. They held him in the water for 2 hours until they were satisfied he would never be white again. They called him Abraham Moses Johnson and his mug shots showed an Afro-American youth of 19 years old. His finger prints were those of Abraham; not Billy. Sentenced to life without parole, he was allocated a cell in the block held for black prisoners; C Block. Now he had to learn to live black, but a chance comes for him to escape and he manages to get to a farm house owned by an old Negro who decides to look after him and protect him.

My Date with Destiny book 1 - During the early 70's the New South Wales Government enacted a law against Gay Men and the sexual act of Buggery. Many men got caught up in this witch hunt and few survived unscathed. David was an apprentice Motor Mechanic and had met Jacko; a builders labourer and they shared a flat together. Early one morning their flat was raided by the local police and both he and Jacko were charged under Section 78 and 79 of the Criminal Code; for buggery and sex with another man. David swore to learn all about the law whilst in prison and to fight this injustice. The story takes you through the plight of the 78'ers and their fight to overturn the law, but in trying, David was seriously injured in an attack in prison and receives spinal injuries relegating him to a wheel chair.

My Date with Destiny book 2 – David is released from prison with a degree in law and starts his fight against the injustices of the New South Wales Criminal convictions of Gay men. He is appointed to the Commission for Wrongful Convictions and his investigations uncover plots within the prison system and high up in politics involving the Russian KGB and Russian Mafia. There is an attempt on his life but Jacko manages to convince the KGB leader in Australia to kidnap David and send him to Russia and away from their operations in Australia. Jacko was a sleeper agent for the KGB.

My Date with Destiny book 3 – David and Jacko escape Ratne where they were held as workers in a new town being built near the border of the Ukraine and Russia. They travel with help from Jacko's blood mother to Turkey where they are met by a representative of MI6. They have secrets to trade for a simple life in Ireland, but life is never simple when MI6 and the KGB work together.

Death Squad - The Presidency – A conglomerate of big business is formed to assassinate the President of the United States should the wrong President be elected to office. A squad of professional killers are formed to carry out the assassination when ordered.

Death Squad 2 – Cuba – Luca is sent to Cuba to restore the family back to its original position as the strongest underworld family in Cuba. Luca takes his Death Squad with him and finally manages to kill all the other drug lords in Havana and take over their territories.

Am I Gay – This is not a story; nor is it a scientific research book. It is a guide to young men who are undecided as to their sexuality. It gives a short rundown of what it is to be a gay man; its pitfalls and enjoyments. It outlines the needs and requirements of a gay man as opposed to being heterosexual. It does not try to be glamorous but does lay out what another gay man has also gone through to be who he is right now. It also lays out the path for a youth in determining his future in the workplace.

Occult

The Devil's Seed – Book 1 – The Devil comes to a young farm worker at the instant of death and offers him immortality in return for his devotion and spreading his word.

The Devil's Seed – Book 2 – A continuation of book 1 and the Devil's Seed is spread throughout Europe.

Skinhead Books

Daniel – A skinhead finds himself kidnapped and forced into slavery but when his owner dies, he finds his freedom once again.

The Fighting Dog – A skinhead becomes a porn star and is then kidnapped and taken overseas. His partner searches for him and finds him but he is not the man he once knew.

A Matter of Honour – A skinhead is placed in a juvenile prison but agrees to report on an inmate to have his record expunged.

Retribution – A skinhead marries and they have a child, but they want to get out of Manchester and the city environment. His wife is killed in a car accident and his son seriously injured and now disabled. He goes after the driver and his passenger when the court gives them a small fine.

Life's Journey book 1, 2, 3, 4, 5 and complete – The story of Jonny; a skinhead youth and his fall into prostitution and murder.

Murder Mysteries

The Detective O'Neil Murder Mysteries – Spiders of my mind – O'Neil delves into the evidence and finds anomalies, so decided to delve a little deeper into the death of 4 medical students.

The Detective O'Neil Murder Mysteries – The Spirit of Joe – Joe is attacked and suffers serious head injuries so is placed into an induced coma. While in the coma he has several 'Out of Body' experiences and finds he is suspected of 3 murders. O'Neal investigates and finds a cult at the University who carry out assassinations as part of their own out of body experiences.

Slavery

Searching for Jefferson - No job, no money and a baby child, Jefferson hits the road to find work when the whole country is looking for work. It's the early 30's and the Stock Market Crash of 1929 and 1931 had destroyed the economy of the USA. Jefferson found work; but not what he had been told. He was made a slave to a brothel and then sold to business owners as cheap manual labour.

My Choice, my Hell – A 3 month paid term in prison turns into a 10 year sentence including working on a chain gang and being sentenced to lethal injection; commuted to life slavery; but the human mind is ingenious and escape is always possible.

My Life in Chains – Kidnapped by a rebel gang in Turkey and then sold into slavery, an archaeology student learns to be a slave to his new Master, but is finally bought by a Middle Eastern Prince and becomes his head of security and saves his Master's life several times.

A Trip to hell – Book 1, 2, 3 and complete – Two men travel to Egypt on a trip after completing their University Degrees, but are kidnapped and made into 'Man Animals' for use as beasts of burden at a quarry. This story tells of their rescue and subsequent slavery after being found by their original owners.

Science Fiction

Ash Cloud Freeze – The volcanoes of the Pacific Rim explode into life causing an ash cloud to circle the earth and cause an ash cloud freeze sending Australia and many other south of the equator countries into a permanent freeze. Governments fall and the military take over the running of the country. Australia becomes a military dictatorship and segregates the people into 3 groups; Freemen, Workers and slaves. But where there is tyranny there is always resistance and this story deals with how the country resists the military.

Deep Sea Rig – A Bacterium is released when a drill ship is searching for oil deposits on the north Western Australian coast. The bacterium is prehistoric and deadly to any living flesh. It is a race against time to kill the Bacterium before it kills every living organism in Australia and maybe the world.

XMM-47 – Extreme Mind Management is a top secret experiment to find out if the mind can be totally controlled through a small brain implant and information fed into the brain. It was funded by the military to help improve the usefulness of the ordinary soldier. Subjects used for the human trials show up faults with the system and the development team are sacrificed to maintain the secrecy.

The Mandarinni Connection – The history of this Planet Earth is littered with great men and their past feets. But were they from Earth or from advanced civilisations from across the Universe? This story takes history and its great men of action and proposes a different story of their lives; takes their beginnings to a new life form made to inhabit peacefully with existing man of the time. Ancient civilisations show rock carvings and early painting of men in space suits; does that give credence to this fictional story? Can early man coexist with technology far superior to its own? Who did build Khufu's pyramid and the pyramids of ancient Mayan temples?

Hole in Time – A Science Fiction story of a youth who accidentally falls through a hole in time and becomes his ancestors. He lives their lives and learns their stories and skills but finds his real heritage is as an Aboriginal. He becomes a leader of Aboriginal people in Tasmania hell bent on restoring his people to their rightful place in the island.

General Fiction

Not Black, Not White – Born from a black woman and a white father, Barnum lived his boyhood secluded in the bush with his mother until he reached his early teens. Half casts were not wanted in the Aboriginal community and the white establishment wanted them taken from their mothers and educated at Mission Schools. His mother had run into the bush when the white people came for her son. A fictitious story about the 'Stolen Generation'.

The Blizzard – This story is about the interaction of 2 men during a heavy blizzard as they are trapped together in a small log cabin in Colorado. It has an unusual twist to the ending.

The Diary of Errol Harbuckle – Errol marries above him and his father-in-law is determined to rid the family of Errol so plots against him and finally has him jailed for embezzlement; a trumped up charge. On release from prison, Errol swears vengeance on all involved with his imprisonment.

Death Squad book 1 – A large conglomerate does not like what it sees for the future of politics in the USA and forms a

Death Squad to rid it of any President that goes against its agenda.

Bully Boy – Life in the mid north of England after WWII and the underworld of crime and corruption.

A Ruined Life – A young man's fight to survive a long prison sentence for a crime he did not commit; and the company he had to keep to do so. A story of survival ruled by the Aryan Brotherhood.

The Alleyway – The late 19th century and early 20th century saw many immigrants arrive on the shores of the USA; most arrived in New York. Landlords took advantage of this seething mass of people and rented their squalid tenements to several families to even one room. We follow the story of one of these immigrants from Ireland; Michael O'Malley.

The Marquis of Death – An historical fiction of a young boy who decides he will take the title of Marquis from his two older uncles. His life becomes a tangle or murder, assassinations and thievery. He becomes a confidant of King Charles II and carries out secret pest control of his enemies.

Adult fairy Tales

The Swine Herder – Merlin takes on an apprentice but the apprentice becomes greedy and wants to become the Wizard of the King's Court. The King; Arthur Pendragon, announces a tournament to decide who is the Grand Wizard of the Land. Merlin decides that if he should win he would spare his adversary but use his powers to make him into 'The Swine Herder'. His Apprentice decides death is the only way to secure his win.

Non Fiction

8 days in Accra – A travel book of my journey to 5 continents, 11 countries in 5 weeks.

Diapers and the fetish of Infantilism

Diaper Stories – a collection of short stories about diapers and those that wear them.

Diaper Stories II Revised – A collection of short stories and a novelette about Diapers and those that wear them.

I Hated Diapers – Because of an infection a young man has to wear a diaper for 3 months, but when his problem is fixed, he finds he needs to continue wearing. He meets a girl who also wears diapers and they have 4 children.

My Diapered Life - Through devious ways, his older siblings cause him to have to wear a diaper 24/7 and he continues to wear throughout his life. His diapered partner is killed in a motor vehicle accident and he begins the search once again for his spiritual partner in life.

Printed in Great Britain
by Amazon